North-East England
PANORAMAS

JEFF HEADS

MYRIAD

LONDON

CONTENTS

Photograph: Hadrian's Wall looking east from above Hotbank Crags
towards Broomlee Lough, with Sewingshields Crags beyond

NORTH NORTHUMBERLAND

A region of wide open countryside, unspoiled beaches and a national park, 'The Secret Kingdom' has a history of border warfare and a wealth of spectacular castles. The holy island of Lindisfarne, the 'cradle of English Christianity', is one of the gems along the area's magnificent coastline

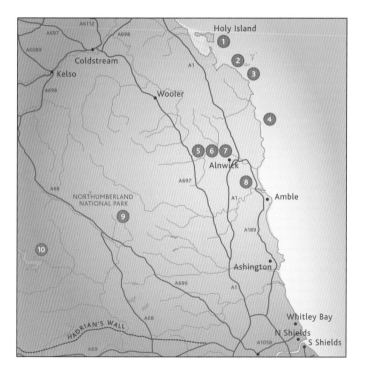

OPPOSITE – ALNWICK CASTLE
Home to the Earls and Dukes of Northumberland since 1309

LINDISFARNE CASTLE, HOLY ISLAND

Holy Island, sometimes known by its older name of Lindisfarne, is situated just off the Northumberland coast, a few miles south of the Scottish border. The island is only accessible by a three-mile long causeway at low tide. Steeped in history, Holy Island was the site of the first Viking invasions of Britain. It is both the birthplace of Anglo-Saxon Britain and of English Christianity. Lindisfarne Castle, seen here on the left, sits on top of a volcanic mound known as Beblowe Craig. The castle was built in the 1550s by Henry VIII, using stones from the nearby demolished priory. In the middle of the horizon are the Farne Islands; to the right, Bamburgh Castle can be seen on the mainland.

BAMBURGH CASTLE

Once the 7th-century capital of the Kingdom of Northumbria, the small coastal village of Bamburgh is dominated by its 11th-century castle. Perched high on an outcrop of the Great Whin Sill, overlooking the North Sea, the castle has been extensively restored, first by Lord Crewe, Bishop of Durham, in the 1750s and then again at the end of the 19th century by Lord Armstrong. Still owned by the Armstrong family, the castle enjoys superb coastal views over dunes and golden sands out towards Holy Island and the Farne Islands.

BAMBURGH BEACH AND THE FARNE ISLANDS

The Northumberland coastline boasts some of the most beautiful and unspoiled beaches in Britain. A succession of sandy bays are fringed by dunes stabilised by windswept marram grass. This photograph, taken from the dunes above Bamburgh beach, shows the Farne Islands to the right. The islands, which can be reached by boat trips from Seahouses harbour, are home to thousands of seabirds and the only east coast breeding ground of the grey seal.

DUNSTANBURGH CASTLE

The ruins of Dunstanburgh Castle sit in a superb natural defensive position perched on steep cliffs, which drop down to the North Sea. Built in 1314 by Thomas, Earl of Lancaster, the castle is situated between the coastal villages of Craster and Embleton. It can be reached by a grassy path which runs between the two villages and which follows the coastline. During the Wars of the Roses Dunstanburgh Castle was a Lancastrian stronghold, but by Tudor times it was in ruins having suffered severe damage from gunfire. Despite its condition the castle still remains an imposing sight.

ALNWICK CASTLE

Alnwick is the second largest inhabited castle in England and is often known as the 'Windsor of the North'. Viewed here from the banks of the River Aln, it has been the home of the earls and dukes of Northumberland since it was bought by Henry Percy in 1309. The castle, which is still lived in by the present Duke and Duchess of Northumberland, continues to dominate the picturesque market town of Alnwick, especially since the opening of the Alnwick Garden within the castle grounds. Already a popular tourist attraction, the castle has increased its visitor numbers since it was used for part of the filming of the Harry Potter films.

GRAND CASCADE, ALNWICK GARDEN

The Duchess of Northumberland's dream of turning a derelict piece of land within the grounds of Alnwick Castle into a beautiful public garden became reality when the Alnwick Garden was officially opened in October 2002 by its patron, HRH the Prince of Wales. This is the Grand Cascade, the largest water feature of its kind in the UK, which forms the centrepiece of the entire garden. The water display has four sequences which change every half-hour throughout the day. These sequences are computer-controlled in two pump rooms situated beneath the cascade.

THE TREE HOUSE, ALNWICK GARDEN

One of the most unique features of the 40-acre Alnwick Garden is its treehouse. With trees appearing to poke through it from every angle, this turreted wooden structure covers an area of almost 6,000 sq ft and is one of the largest treehouses in the world. The north-east has many fine examples of modern architecture but this is surely the quirkiest!

WARKWORTH CASTLE

On a steep hill, within a loop of the River Coquet, this imposing castle looks down upon the main street of Warkworth village. Originally built in the first part of the 12th century it formed part of the chain of defence, along with Bamburgh and Alnwick, against the Scots. The castle was taken over by the Percy family, the Dukes of Northumberland, in 1332. An unusually-shaped keep was added in 1390 and other major additions and alterations followed in the 14th and 15th centuries. With the Percy family choosing Alnwick Castle as their main residence, Warkworth suffered as a consequence. The sides not naturally defended by the steep hill have a moat, as can be seen here, to strengthen its defences. The opening scene of Shakespeare's *Henry IV Part II* is set within the castle which is now looked after by English Heritage.

WINTER'S GIBBET

A not so welcoming sight on the border of the Northumberland National Park, an area of outstanding and varied natural beauty, is Winter's Gibbet. A reminder of more violent times, the body of William Winter was hung here in 1791 after he was found guilty of the murder of Margaret Crozier of the nearby village of Elsdon.The present replica gibbet was erected on the site of the original, at the foot of which is a large block of stone. This is thought to be the base of a Saxon cross, Stang Cross, which marked the highest point on what was then a drovers road. Cattle bred in Scotland were driven along this road to more lucrative markets in England.

KIELDER WATER

Kielder Water is the largest artificial lake in northern Europe. Opened in 1982, having been created by the construction of a dam in the upper part of the North Tyne valley, it has a surface area of 2,684 acres (1086ha) and a shoreline perimeter of 27 miles (43km). As well as providing water supplies for Tyneside, Wearside and Teesside it also offers facilities for all types of watersports and angling. Surrounded by Kielder Forest, the area's unique habitat supports a wide variety of wildlife.

SOUTH NORTHUMBERLAND

Hadrian's Wall runs through the middle of this area of beautiful countryside with its open moorland and picturesque towns and villages. Pretty market towns such as Hexham and Corbridge trace their history back to Roman times

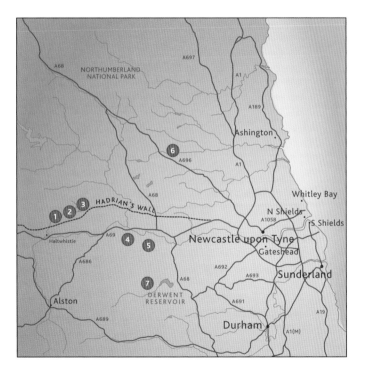

OPPOSITE – CORBRIDGE
A vital bridging point on the Tyne since Roman times

CAW GAP, HADRIAN'S WALL

Hadrian's Wall is the country's most famous reminder of the 400-year Roman occupation of Britain. It marked the northern boundary of their empire and stretched from Bowness-on-Solway on the west coast, to Wallsend on the east coast. The wall, in most places 7-8 feet wide, was begun in AD122 at the command of the Emperor Hadrian (AD 117-138) to separate the Romans from the 'Barbarians'. This view shows the sun setting behind a section of the wall at Caw Gap.

STEEL RIGG, HADRIAN'S WALL

This view of Hadrian's Wall, looking east from Steel Rigg towards Crag Lough with the wall still visible in the distance as it disappears over the summit toward Hotbank Crags, shows how the Romans used the natural defences of the landscape to their full advantage. In the dip in the foreground is one of the many milecastles that can be found along the length of the wall, together with forts, temples and turrets. There are also many museums, visitor centres and reconstructions all of which demonstrate what life was like for the Roman soldiers guarding the wall almost 2,000 years ago.

CRAG LOUGH, HADRIAN'S WALL

Hadrian's Wall traverses some of the most breathtaking countryside in England. With the recent opening of Hadrian's Wall Path, the country's newest National Trail, walkers can now follow the path along the wall and enjoy many spectacular views. This photograph shows one of the most stunning sections of the path as it passes high above Crag Lough.

HEXHAM

This busy Northumberland market town dates from the 7th century and is situated near the junction of the North Tyne and South Tyne rivers. This view shows Hexham House Gardens and Hexham Abbey. Much of the present abbey was built in the 12th century. However, some of the original work still exists, such as the Saxon crypt, which was partly built with stones from the remains of the nearby Roman fort of Corstopitum.

CORBRIDGE

This small town is sited on the north bank of the River Tyne and developed from the Roman town of Corstopitum, a garrison town for the nearby section of Hadrian's Wall. The site marked the strategically important point where Dere Street, the Roman road running between York and Edinburgh, crossed the Stanegate, which ran westwards to Carlisle. The narrow single-file bridge, still used today, dates from 1674. At 160 yards (146m) long, its seven arches span the River Tyne. It was the only bridge across the Tyne to survive the terrible flood of 1771.

WALLINGTON HALL

Set in 100 acres of gardens, lakes and woodlands, Wallington Hall dates back to 1688. It is located south of the village of Cambo, which was originally built in 1740 to house the workers on the Wallington Estate. The Hall is now owned by the National Trust and, among its many treasures, is famous for its murals depicting scenes of Northumberland's history. Wallington is also noted for its grounds and gardens, parts of which were laid out by Capability Brown who was educated at the school in Cambo.